Where and How to sell Greeting Cards

To purchase copies or obtain reprint rights contact:
Thomas R Roth Jr
149 Wylie St
Chester SC 29706
Phone -803-377-7680

Email -sales @missingtoepublishing.com

ISBN-13: 9780692649107
ISBN-10:0692649107

Contents

What This Book is Not About   5
Product Preparation   13

Sales Preparation   20
Mental and Spiritual Preparation   23
1.   Marketing Budget   32
2.   Marketing Calendar   39
Brick and Mortar Stores 41
Online 42
Chain Stores   42

Mass Merchandisers   42
Farmers Market   44

Flea market 45
Craft and Art Shows   46

Card Parties   47
Create a Card Club via Direct Mail   48
Corporate Sales 51
4.   Wholesale   54
Florist 54
Dog Groomers 55
Pet and Feed Stores   55
Veterinarian   56
Restaurants   57
Gas stations   58
Convenience Store   59
Drug Stores   59
Gift Shops   60

Arts Councils   61

5.   Book Stores   62

6.   A word about selling local   62

7.   Selling on the World Wide Web   66

Methods of selling on the web   66

8.   Promotion on the world wide web   67

9.   You Fulfill the orders 71

ETSY   71

Amazon Handmade   73

Your own web site   73

Facebook   75

Someone Else fulfills the orders 76

Greeting Card Universe 76

Zazzle, Cafe Press and others   78

Fine Art America   79

10.   Chain Stores   82

11.   Mass Merchandisers 85

Where and How to Sell Your Greeting Cards.

What This Book is Not About

This is not a book about making cards. This book is not about the correct colors or the right words. This book is not about paper, ink or printing. This book is not about who buys greeting cards. This book is not about any design skills needed. This book is not about the software to create cards

This book is about selling greeting cards. This book is about the companies that purchase greeting cards. This book is about making sales to those companies. This book is about building a greeting card business. This book is about opportunities. If you want to increase your sales, create strong relationships, and be a supplier of greeting cards then this is the book for you.

About The Author

I have been a photographer for well over forty years. During these forty plus years I have seen a lot of change in both the photography, printing, and the greeting cards industry. These changes have made it easier to enter these industries and increased the competition.

For over thirty years I have been a wholesaler of floral products including cards. I started at the bottom of the floral industry and ended up owning a wholesale Florist. During those thirty three years I learned how to sell. Selling is the key to any business. No sales equals no business.

I have been selling greeting cards for well over twenty years. I started selling cards long before the age of computers and the internet The biggest difference from when I started selling cards and now is the addition of computers. Again, computers have made it easier to enter the market and created more ways to market a product.

There is one constant from when I first stated making greeting cards and now, and that is selling. No mater how great a card maker you are very little will happen if you do not go out and make sales. To be successful is this business requires that you know how to make a sale and who to make a sale to.

Introduction

Welcome to an Eight-billion-dollar market. Over six and one half billion cards were sold last year in the United States alone. That is great news for any and all inspiring card producers. Sure there are some big players in the industry, but there is still plenty of room for you and me to sell and make a profit from the greeting card industry. Let us look at some interesting facts from the Greeting Card Association.

•   The most popular Everyday card-sending occasion by far is Birthday, followed by a number of secondary occasions that include Sympathy, Thank You, Wedding, Thinking of You, Get Well, New Baby and Congratulations.

•   The most popular Seasonal cards are Christmas cards, with some 1.6 billion units purchased (including boxed cards). This is followed by cards for Valentine's Day (145 million units, not including classroom valentines), Mother's Day (133 million units), Father's Day (90 million units), Graduation (67 million units), Easter (57 million units), Halloween (21 million units), Thanksgiving (15 million units) and St. Patrick's Day (7 million units).

•   Women purchase an estimated 80% of all greeting cards. Women spend more time choosing a card than men, and are more likely to buy several cards at once.

Preparation

- Greeting card prices can vary from 50 cents to $10 – with a price point for every consumer. The vast majority are between $2 and $4. (Total price per year include boxed cards.) The cost of a typical counter card, however, is between $2 and $4. Cards featuring special techniques, intricate designs and new technologies and innovations – such as the inclusion of sound chips and LED lights – as well as handmade cards, are at the top of the price scale.

- Seven out of 10 card buyers surveyed consider greeting cards "absolutely" or "almost" essential to them. Eight out of 10 of these buyers expect their purchases to remain the same going forward. Of the balance, twice as many card buyers say they will "increase" their purchasing as say they will "decrease" their purchasing in the coming year.

- Younger card buyers and those who are more technology savvy are currently the ones most engaged in buying paper greeting cards online.

- Most people now acknowledge many more birthdays than ever before because of Facebook, but they aren't necessarily sending fewer cards as a result.

- The tradition of giving greeting cards as a meaningful expression of personal affection for another person is still being deeply ingrained in today's youth, and this tradition will likely continue as they become adults and become responsible for managing their own important relationships.

The statistics copied from the Greeting Card Association's

website you can see that the future is very exciting for those that want to be a producer in the card business.

So where do you start? It starts with a passion for creating cards that people will want to buy and share with their friends. Sometimes this can be as simple as just one card, or as complex as an entire line of ten or more cards.

Once you have cards that you are happy with, it is time to reach out into the world and get your cards into the hands of the buying public. That is where this book can help. This book is all about selling greeting cards. Where and how to give you the best chance of letting the public see what you can help them say. Let's get started.

"Chance favors the prepared mind"

Louis Pasteur

The title of this section is called preparation but could be called goal setting for my greeting card company. Being prepared to take your company and your-self to the next level is the first step. Some of my goals are:

- Sale more greeting cards

- Teach others to sell more cards

- Spend more time as photographer making greeting cards

- Make some money

When you have a clear reason why you want to be a greeting producer and distributor, then you can begin to create a successful business. With decisive goals, you can now begin to prepare to win.

Preparation is divided into three sections, product, sales and marketing, and mental preparation. I cannot stress enough the importance of this first step. Without a solid foundation it is very difficult to make sales.

Product Preparation

Product is the first step that most of us take in starting a greeting card company. Without cards there is no company. But lets us take the preparation step a bit further. Have you considered all the possibilities and how to handle them? Here is the list I come up with:

- Single cards or card sets?

- Cello wrap or none?

- Box type…. cardboard, clear plastic, black, white, or gold?

- One size card or multiple sizes?

- How many cards per box?

- Mixed cards in a box or all one type?

- Display type?

- Products for presentation?

- Pricing single card retail?

- Pricing cards boxed?

- Pricing wholesale?

- Minimum Quantities on wholesale?

- What should the back of my card say?

- Do I need an order form?

Have I missed anything? If I did add it to the list. The answers to these question will help you in your quest to become a card distributor.

Let us start with the simplest problem to solve and that is what to say on the back of the card. There is no rule that I have found about what to print on the back of a card. I have seen some cards with extremely little written on their back and I have seen others that tell a complete story of their card business, with everything in between.

However there is one thing that all cards have on the

back: the name of who provides the card.

On my cards I have used many different styles and words. All my cards have my company name, city, state, phone number, and email address at the bottom. Recently I have been placing a QR code in the middle of the card. The QR code sends people to my website. You can easily create a QR code. Just do a search and you will find many companies that will generate a code for free. I currently use www.qrstuff. com Above the code I place the title of the card. Yes, I title every card. I have learned that is best to title cards because inevitably someone will ask for a title.

What to put on the back of your cards is up to you. Experiment until you find a formula that you are comfortable with.

Another issue I had to face is what size card to offer. This does not sound like it should be much of a problem until you look at the many different sizes that the competition is offering. Sizes range from just a couple inches square to some that are two or three feet in size and everything in-between. There are some standard sizes that most printers offer and the most common is five by seven inches, also know as A7 paper.

My first cards were printed on 5x7 stock and I still do so today, but I have added a smaller size to sell as boxed sets. I choose another standard size called A6 which is 4.5x6.25 inches and they are the cards I use in boxed sets.

I have just added a new size to my mix. It is a square card that folds to five inches by five inches. This is a new format for me. The square size works well for my thank-you sales. It is smaller than most cards and folks seem to like that in a thank you card.

How many cards do I put in a boxed set? I have yet to come up with a definitive answer to that question. I still experiment with what is just the right number of cards in a set. There has to be a balance between the number of cards and the selling price. Too many cards and the price is too high. Too few cards and the set looks skimpy. I recommend that you play around with the numbers and find a combination that works.

The last question I had to ask myself about boxed sets is, assorted cards or just one type of card in the box. I do both. However most of my sales are from assorted cards in a box. When I sale assorted cards in a box I like to put a label on the back of the box that shows the assortment of cards in the box.

Pricing is one of the most difficult jobs to accomplish. Before I explain how I figure my prices I need to explain some definitions. I use the term gross mark up. Do not get confused between gross mark up and net profits. If accounting is not one of your strong points, you still need to understand gross mark up. www.accountingcoach.com is a great place to learn about gross mark up and another commonly used phrase cost of goods. When first starting out it may be difficult to determine your true cost of goods but over time and good record keeping it will become much easier. Good accounting software will also make a lot easier to keep track of everything finical.

I figured my pricing by starting at the beginning. I first found the bottom line cost of my cards, envelopes and packaging. I then added my wholesale markup on the cards, and in my case that is a thirty percent gross markup. Why do I use thirty percent? Because thirty percent will cover my cost to do business plus my cost of goods and a profit. In simplest terms, I multiplied my cost by one point five, or, cost $1.00, X, 1.50

markup. The selling price is one dollar and fifty cents per card wholesale. These numbers are for example only and do not represent my cost.

I use the same formula for pricing boxed sets. Number of cards multiplied by the cost per card and envelope plus the cost of box multiplied by one point five zero. Sticking with the numbers from above, the example would look like this, 6 cards per box at a cost of $1.00 per card equals $6.00 plus the cost of the box at $1.00 equals $7.00. The wholesale selling cost would then be $7.00 multiplied by 1.50 which equals $10.50 per boxed set.

Theses are the numbers that I use when calculating my prices, you may choose a different method. What ever method you choose to value your cards, create a system. A good pricing in place will let you quickly determine the selling value of a card.

Now that I have my wholesale cost I can have a recommended retail price. Most retailers like the idea of doubling their cost. On the example above the recommended retail price would be three dollars per card. However they may not mark up boxed cards in quite the same way. In this case I would recommend the retail of the boxed sets from the above example sell for around seventeen dollars a box. These are only recommendations and I would never insist that a shop owner sell for that price. If the shop would like to sell for more or less that is their provocative.

Display is another area that you need to consider. There are many options to choose from. Plastic, wood, metal, and cardboard are some of the options. Size,footprint, pockets, vertical or horizontal are some other options to be added to the mix and, of course their expense.

Let us take a second and explain some of the definitions used in this segment. The first term is "spinner." This type of display allows you to display more cards by allowing the display to spin around. Spinner displays cannot go flush against a wall. They need to be out in the open to function properly. Some spinners sit on the floor and others are made to sit on a table. The second term I use is called the display footprint. A footprint is the amount of space that the display requires. Displays that do not spin require less space than ones that do. Our final term is "pockets." Pockets are the individual card holders on a stand. Pockets size and the number of pockets can vary. Pockets can be vertical or horizontal. So how do you choose?

I choose to go with three different types and sizes of displays. The most expensive and the largest is called a floor spinner. The one I choose is a metal product but there are also spinners made of wood, and acrylic. These floor spinners can hold hundreds of cards and are slim and do not take up too much of a footprint. These types of stands are designed to stand on their own. Pocket size and the number of pockets per stand can vary.

My second display choice was called a table top spinner. These spinners also come in many types of materials. This type of stand is designed to sit on a table or display block. They are half the size of a floor spinner and can display hundreds of cards. Their size and number of pockets can vary. They can also have a mix of both horizontal and vertical cards or just one type of orientation. Both the floor spinner and the table top spinner are best suited for retail stores.

My third choice of display is called a counter top display. It is much smaller than a table top spinner and does not spin. This type of display is made to sit on the counter where people pay the bills. Most of these displays have no more than four pockets but can still hold fifty or so cards. This type of display works well in restaurants, gas stations, and pet groomers.

So far I have talked about display for single card sales, but I also wanted to sell boxed sets of cards and other types of stationary. Displays for these kinds of items are different then floor spinners and counter top displays. In most cases you will need help from your customer to display boxed sets and more. Shelf space can be limited and it is best that you discuss your needs with owner.

Another word in the display of boxed card sets is information on the back of the box. Just like with the back of a card what to say is entirely up to you. If you sale assorted cards in a box, I have found that you will have better sales if you place a label on the back of the box with pictures of the assortment of cards. This will accomplish two things. One is it lets the customer know that there is more then one type of card in the box. The second is that it will cut down on shrinkage because customer will not have to open the box to see the assortment. What you choose should be well thought out and add to the packaging.

Now we are getting somewhere. I have my prices set and my display options chosen. It is time now to prepare for making sales.

Sales Preparation

Sales preparation brings with it another round of decisions to make. Such as:

- How best to present my cards to potential clients?

- Do I need business cards?

- What type of promotional material do I need?

- What should my promotional material say?

- Should I have a business phone and number?

- Should I have a toll free number?

- Should I have a separate fax number?

- What are my sales terms?

I choose two ways to present my cards as a wholesaler. One way was to display individual cards in a leather book with pages to hold cards. The leather added a nice touch and using clear plastic pages made a nice presentation. The leather book is the three ring binder type and allows me to easily change cards in and out. Adding a divider between themes allows to quickly get to the cards that the customer would be interested in.

The second method for presenting cards to a potential customer is simple. The cards are in boxed sets and I just bring one in of each set and put them down on the table.

When I am selling a small display, I like to present the entire package. I present the display fully load with cards and ready to sell. All the customer do is place the display on the counter or table and their job is over. Why do I do this? This type of presentation eliminates the need for the shop keeper to work. Less work is always a great selling point.

Promotional material is a wide open subject and because it is so wide open there are lots of options to chose from. I go more into depth with this subject in the section devoted to promotion.

Terms of sale is a subject that you should be familiar with. There are many different terms in the business world but there are five that I think you need to consider.

- Prepayment

- Cash on Delivery

- Deposit with balance due on delivery

- Net thirty days

- Consignment

I have listed these in the order in which I ask for payment. I am always prepared to ask for payment up front. If I can not get payment up front then my next option is cash on delivery. Most of the time cash on delivery are the terms I end up with.

If I receive an order that is extremely large I am up

front with the customer and explain that I appreciate their order I will need some help on producing their products. At this time I will ask for a deposit with the balance due on delivery or in thirty days. Most customers understand and are willing to help. Do not be afraid to ask.

Consignment is having a customer sell your cards and not pay you for them until after they are sold. In many shops this may be the only way to get in the door. I like consignment in many places because that allows me to set prices and have control over the product. Consignment can benefit both you and the shop owner. The shop owner gets a product to sell that they do not pay for until it is sold, you get exposure and sales. Win win.

Mental and Spiritual Preparation

Mental and spiritual preparation is where you pull it all together. This is where your goals become important. Some thoughts to consider when preparing for a selling appointment.

- What type of client am I going to see?

- Do they have more than one location?

- What kind of cards should I present?

- How much sales volume can I expect?

- What kind of offer am I going to start with?

- Should I ask for a down payment?

- What kind of terms am I willing to accept?

- Have I thought about the questions the prospective client might ask?

- Why do I want my cards in this clients store?

Some of the items on the above list will not take a lot of time to answer. However they are extremely important to answer before you try to sell to anyone. I suggest you give much thought to each of theses questions and have answers embedded in your head, this may mean the difference between making a sale and not. I can not count the number of times I have been frustrated because the salesperson could not answer questions about a product. DO NOT BE THAT KIND OF A PERSON!

I hope that you have done your research before you walk into the customers place of business. You should know how many locations, size of the locations, and the type of products they sell. You should also have some type of an idea of how much sales volume to expect. When first starting out this may difficult to determine.

If you have your research completed, it will not be a problem to have your card selection and offer ready before you walk in the door. A little bit of research can go a long way into making a sale. Remember that business owners are busy people and do not have time to waste listening to ramble about your card line. Br firm, friendly and straight to the point.

One of the more difficult question to come to terms with is should, "I ask for a down payment." Talking money scares a lot of people including me. In almost all cases I ask for a deposit of at least thirty percent and more often fifty percent, with the balance cash on delivery or C.O.D. Does this always work? No but it never hurts to ask. I have never had anyone complain because I asked for a deposit.

Size does matter. When I have been hit with a large order from a new customer I will ask for a deposit or at the least cash on delivery. It pays to have the answer to questions like this before you head out to see a client. There is no set rule on what terms to ask from a customer, so why not start with asking for payment in full before you ship the order and if that is not suitable with the client then ask what kind of terms would be suitable for them. Sometimes you may have to walk away and say no.

The last question on the list for mental preparation is, "why do I want my cards in this business" this the most important question of all to know the answer. The answer to this question may be the reason to making a sale. Knowing the answer to this question creates the passion needed to make a sale. When you have the "why" then most everything else will fall into place. The more "whys"' you have the greater chance you have of making a sale and becoming a greeting card producer, and distributor. Her are some possible whys I might want to sell cards to a company.

- I want more sales.

- Your company fits the type of cards I produce.

- You cater to local vendors.

- My cards are location specific and you are in the area that the cards made are for.

- Their customers have asked for cards.

- I create my cards to raise awareness of a cause and your company supports the cause.

Here are at least six reason why I want to business with a certain company. How hard do you think it is to make a sale to that company?

I can not stress enough to make a list of whys for each company that you want to do business with. When a customer is aware of your reasons to do business with them, it is easy to close the sale.

When making an offer to a prospective client, I taylor make sales pitch to meet the customer's needs. I educate the customer on why my cards makes sense in their stores, and then I ask for the sale.

Make customer acquisition a system. Strive to always be on the look out for your next customer. When you have a system for getting customers then you can measure your effectiveness. In the section I discuss software that can assist in customer acquisition an maintenance easier. When you can measure your effectiveness then you know when and where to make changes, and you can improve.

I hope that you can see the value in through preparation. Good planning can eliminate a lot of problems before you ever try to sell your first card. Thinking out your process of obtaining customers is only the first step in becoming a greeting card distributor. Let us continue and get some customers.

A little bit about selling

"It is your attitude not your aptitude
that determines your altitude"

Zig Ziglar

Selling a product and yourself is not an easy objective to accomplish. Add to the negative stereo types that come with salespersons and it is no wonder that selling creates a lot of anxiety in people. Do not despair. Selling is a skill that can be learned.

If you are new to selling or you just need some help I recommend that you study Zig Ziglar's book Sell Your Way to the Top. Zig will explain that you do not need any special skills to become a top sales person.

Another book that I recommend is Jeffery Gitomer's Little Red Book on Selling. In his book Jeffery help you overcome the fears associated with selling. A must read for all people involved in the selling process.

In my forty plus years of selling I have developed an acronym that I teach to inspiring sales people, PET. If you can remember this when approaching a client you have a great chance of making a sale.

Pet stands for, passion, enthusiasm, and take action. These three simple things will make you an outstanding sales person.

Passion is the first step to being good at anything. It takes passion to create a great greeting card and it takes passion to sell a greeting card. Passion comes from inside. You can't buy it. You can't hire someones passion. It has to come from within you. You have to want to be a greeting card sales person. You have to be consumed with the thought that you can have your cards in a particular store.

What does passion bring to the sales table. It is passion that creates desire. Desire is fundamental to selling. It is desire that helps you walk through the door. Without desire you will have a hard time making any sale. Customers can sense when you desire to do business with them.

Enthusiasm is an off shoot of passion. When you enthusiastic about what you have created and your desire to sell that card to the public, it will be difficult for a buyer to say no. Enthusiasm is at it's basic level is excitement. When you are excited it shows. It is hard for a customer to say no when you are excited.

Enthusiasm is catchy. When you are enthusiastic others around you become excited. Your team becomes enthusiastic. Your customer becomes excited about what you are trying to accomplish. In the selling world, nothing beats an enthusiastic customer.

The finial step of the PET analogy is T for take action. This is a most crucial step. Taking action is what will make the sale. Action is required to prepare, and walk through the door. Action is what will get you in front of the customer. Action is what it is needed to close the sale. Action is what makes you a outstanding sales person..

Action can also create momentum. When you take

those first steps in selling you will find it is easier to take the next step. Only action will can create momentum and momentum can take you a long way in your sales adventure.

Action is where most sales people fall short. They allow fears stop them. They lost their passion. They are no longer enthusiastic, and it will show.

As with many of the instructions in this book, create a system for selling your greeting cards. When there is a system in place then you can manage and make corrections as you move along. A system also helps eliminate many fears that are associated with selling.

My final words about selling is it is all about attitude. To quote Zig Ziglar; "It is your attitude not your aptitude that determines your altitude." Approach selling as the fun part of your business. Too many people consider selling as a necessary evil. There is nothing evil about selling. Keep your attitude positive, passionate, enthusiastic and you will have great success in your greeting card business.

Promotion

The old saying that it takes money to make money is still true. How ever it no longer takes a large bank account to be a gorilla marketer. I am a big believer in gorilla marketing.

The biggest mistake I and others have made is failing to make a plan. Planing is the most important part of any promotional strategy. Failing to plan is planing to fail. There are thousands of choices to make when planing a promotional campaign and research is a must. Unless you have an unlimited supply of money, you must make sure that every dollar spent is producing results.

Today's internet offers a host of marketing opportunities and many will let you start for free. I think that it important that you learn areas that need to be the same in the online and off line world. These should include but not limited to:

- Theme

- Branding

- Colors

- Call to Action

- Planning

Most of these sound simple, but are very important in setting up your basic company and are free.

Keep your theme consistent between the off line and online world. I know you are saying to your self that you are not that stupid, just make sure. Company colors are the same as theme. Pick out a palette and stick with the colors on everything you do.

If there is one area that I think is most over looked in the print and internet marketing is the "call to action." Why spend good money on print materials and web advertising if you do not make a call to action. A call to action can be as simple as visit our website or asking for a down payment on a product.

There are several times throughout this book that I mention "customer profile." A customer profile is a must in your plan to sell greeting cards. You need to know the type of customer that you wants to buy your greeting cards.

How do you create a customer profile. Ask questions. Ask questions about the end user of your cards. Ask question about the wholesale accounts you desire to acquire. In the section internet promotion I cover more about building a customer profile.

When planning your marketing make sure to plan for both the web and the print world. Use as much cross over material as possible. Keep the message and theme consistent as possible and always ask the customer to do something.

To keep with the spirit of gorilla marketing I must mention that before you spend any money make sure you have exhausted all of the free marketing weapons available to you.

📁📢 Marketing Budget

It required several tries to produce a budget that I could believe in. The process is not as easy as you might think. The biggest question is "where do I start?" I am sure that not everyone will answer the question the same way, but this is how I developed my marketing budget.

Having set my goals earlier, I knew what I wanted to accomplish. I had researched what others had done and the cost involved. Armed with this information, I broke my budget into three sections, fixed costs, variable cost and sweat equity.

Fixed costs are expenses that are paid to maintain the basic structure of the plan. Without these basics it would be very difficult implement a strong marketing campaign.

Variable costs are expenses that are paid for the most part at my discretion. These expenses are mostly for paid advertising but are not always limited to advertising.

Sweat equity is the cost of the work done to maintain a marketing campaign. I don't get paid to do this work. In many cases there are companies that will do the work for me and may even do a better job, but as guerrilla marketer, I do what I can. You need to decide how much of the work you can do and what part needs to be farmed out. Do a search for the type of work you need done, you will find there are many people that can help and all different price levels.

The biggest mistake when working on a marketing

budget in not creating a system to track results. You have to track the results of the budget to know if you have spent your money in the right direction.

If making a budget is not familiar to you, then your need to stop and learn. It took me several times to come up with a starting budget. I doubt that I will have a budget that looks anywhere close to the budget I have now in a couple of years from now.

My Basic Budget

Budget Month		
Budget Project		
Budget Item	Monthly Cost	
	Fixed Costs	
Websites	$17.00	3 sites
Mail Chimp	10.00	Email
Libsyn	7.00	Podcast
Fine Art America	2.50	
	Sub-total	$39.50
	Variable Costs	
Etsy Fees		
Table at Market	28.00	
Classified Ads		Paid Ads
Google Ads		Paid Ads
Facebook Ads		Paid Ads
7 Search Ads		Paid ads
Free Cards	$10.00	Give A Ways
	Subtotal	$38.00
	Sweat Equity	
Blog		
Podcast Interview		
Website Maintenance		
	Total Investment	$77.50

The heart of the budget is the websites. I maintain three of them. Each site has a different purpose and is targeted towards different clients. Website maintenance can be very time consuming and is best tackled a little bit at a time.

The next item on the budget is "Mail Chimp" and is my email management company. There are many companies that will handle your email collection and sending duties of most any company. I choose "Mail Chimp" because it seemed to be easy and simple to understand and would easily fit my needs. The basic account at "Mail Chimp are free, but I choose to add some advance features which cost ten dollars a month.

The advance feature that I use allows me to send the new email recipient after signing up back to a page that I desire. The unpaid version sends the visitor back to the home page and that is not where I want them to go. This is important because I want the new recipient to stay on my site and read the content.

Item number three is "Libsyn". A podcast hosting company. Currently the seven dollar a month is for tracking traffic and listeners. A very small sum to pay to obtain insight into who's listening to my podcast.

The fourth item under fixed is "Fine Art America." I use FAA as a gallery with the ability to sell fine art prints and greeting cards. FAA lets me set the prices I want and I can offer both originals and prints. Hundreds of companies offer what Fine Art America does but I think FAA does it a little bit better.

The next section of the budget is what I refer to as "variable expenses.". Most of the items in the basic budget are left blank except for the free card section because the amounts spent each month will vary. I have been using cards to pay bills and give a way to prospective customers and the costs stays about the same month after month. Variable expenses are the easiest to tack. Tracking the success or failure of variable expense is the only way to determine where to spend money.

The part of the budget referred to as sweat equity are items that do not require a lot of cash investment but requires a lot of work.

Website maintenance is the most time consuming area of my sweat equity budget. True, I could hire someone to do the job, but I am a guerrilla marketer and do not have the extra money to hire anyone at this time. Even if I had plenty of money to spend, I would still educate myself on how the website functions and allowing me to have a say in how everything works.

Once Mail Chimp is setup, there software helps automate my email sign up process. Setting up Mail Chimp was easy and integration into the site was a simple copy and paste solution. If you are serious about your online marketing, then I recommend an email service of some kind. There are many companies that provide this service. I suggest that you do a search and explore these companies and pick the one that you think fits your needs.

The podcast is more a labor of love then anything. I love to keep learning. One of the best ways to learn is to learn from other people's experiences. I also want to share what I have learned. Writhing this book is one way to share, but the podcast allows me to continuing sharing after the book is published.

The podcast can be time consuming. Not only is there the time involved in recording the podcast there is also behind scenes work that can be even more time consuming.

Once you have finished this book and are ready for more information, tune into the Greeting Cards Evermore podcast, where I try to keep with all the latest tools and trends. The web address is www.greetingcardsevermore.com

Display is one item that is not in the budget. When I sell a customer that needs display equipment, the quote I give the customer includes the price of the display. I never try to make money off the display but I do include the cost of display in my price.

It seems that a blog has become one the tools necessary for promotion. Writing takes time. Good writing takes even more time. Creating and maintaining a blog is not an easy task to accomplish. Try to think out your blog subjects well in advance and write several before starting to post them. There are many resources about writing and maintaining a blog. Do a Google search to learn more.

Even with a budget that is as small as this one, it requires a respect for organization. The only way to get maximum profits from investments is a constant daily involvement. It is too easy to forget what needs to be done in two weeks from now. You need some way to keep track of all your endeavors.

There are many types of applications that can help you manage your marketing. The application I use is free and works across a broad range of devices. It is called "Insightly." The App is one of Google tools that is available free. There is a paid version for as little as $5.00 per month, but I have yet to need the extra goodies.

Insightly is a customer relationship management or customer relationship marketing software and is becoming more important in my daily work flow. The software helps me identify possible opportunities and link all the information about that opportunity in one place. Perhaps I would like to sell to gas stations, as I gather information and people to contact Insightly lets me link all the info together. When the time comes to prepare for selling to a gas station, everything I need is ready in one spot.

The second part that I like about Insightly is it has a task tracking feature. I use this feature every day to keep track of what needs to be done and when. Opportunities can be broken down into small steps and then placed into the calendar making them much easier to accomplish. Use this feature to remember when to renew ads, update your site, keep track of blog posts, and what time that doctors appointment was.

Insightly also has a powerful email feature that will let you schedule emails to be sent out at the time you chose. Insightly also captures all incoming email address making it easy to build your email list.

I would highly recommend Insightly to anyone whom has lots of chores to keep track of and does not want to miss any opportunities.

▤◁͡ Marketing Calendar

A budget does not any good if you don't have a plan. A marking calendar is a blueprint for your marketing activities. It is difficult to build a house without a plan and it is difficult to have an effective marking plan without a marketing calendar. Below is a sample calendar that I use.

Month		Media	Money	Grade
January				
February				
March		Table at market	$28.00	
April		Table at Market	$28.00	
May		Table at market	$28.00	
June				
July				
August				
Sept.				
October				
Nov.		Facebook ads 7search ads Table at market	$28.00	
Dec.				

Most of the headings are fairly straight forward and easy to understand. If more space is needed then I ad additional rows, as with the month of November.

In the space that says message I use a code to refer to the ad that is being tested. I do this only to save space.

Grading is done by measuring the results against the goals or objective that I am trying to achieve. These are the goals and objectives that you set out in the planning stage of your greeting card business. See why planning is so important.

When you have a working budget and calendar you have some powerful weapons to start your greeting card business. You have done your home work. You have prepared yourself to the best of your knowledge. It is time now to go and take action. Time to take what we have learned and prepared for, and put it to use. Nothing can take the place of this step Action is required from here on out to be successful. Action will make you a greeting card creator and distributor. Action can put money in your pockets.

About The List

Brick and Mortar Stores

The title of this group of locations pretty much says it all. These are stores that have a physical presence.

There are two types of locations in this group. The first are places that you are the wholesaler and the retailer. These locations require you to be present.

The second group of locations you are only the wholesaler. You do not need to be present to make sales.

Online
The online world is an ever changing and a growing location for your products. It is well beyond the scope of this book to list all the possibilities. However, I do want to touch on some of the larger sites and sites that are devoted to greeting cards.

Chain Stores
Chain stores are different then the mass merchandisers. Many chains act like large mass merchandisers and in that case you should treat them as such.

Mass Merchandisers
The mass merchandisers are those multiple store chains that tend to dominate the marketplace. This group includes the super mass merchandisers such as Walmart, Target, and CVS. Etc.

Retail

The first four locations on the brick and mortar list are places that you are the wholesaler and retailer. In these cases, you create, produce and distribute directly to the end consumer. When setting your prices and you want to sell wholesale in the future, remember, to sell at a high enough profit so you will still make money at the wholesale level.

Farmers Market

Some of the most fun I have had selling greeting cards has been at the farmer's market. Farmer's markets can vary in size and venue. Some markets are outdoors, but many are also indoors. I have been to some farmer's markets that are several blocks long and others that are in a small parking lot.

Doing business with a farmer's market is fairly easy and in many cases very inexpensive. It is up to you to provide display for your products. There are many ways to display at the farmers market. I would recommend that you try a table top spinner. A floor spinner will work but be aware that the bottom pockets may get dirty.

A wide variety of cards can be sold at the market, and you will know very quickly if your cards fit the type of customers that buy from the market. You will be dealing with the end user and they will let you know if your cards do not met their needs.

Flea market

Some would consider a flea market and a farmer's market the same thing, but there are some differences. At a flea market I find that most of the potential customers are there to find a bargain. Customers at farmer's markets are there because they are concerned with the quality of their food.

The cost to sell at a flea market is small. Some markets provide tables, and some do not. The market that I sell from offers covered tables for ten dollars and uncovered spots with no tables for five dollars. Visit the market that you might want to sell at before you invest your time and money. Look at the volume of buyers. Are they walking away with products or just looking? Talk with some of the vendors and ask how sales are, most of the time you will get an honest answer.

Be prepared to provide display for your product. One word of caution is that flea markets are outdoors and can soil cards quickly. Take precautions to keep your product looking its' best.

All variety of cards can be sold at the market but I have found that seasonal cards sell best.

As I stated above, most buyers are at the flea market to

find a bargain. Can you sell at a price that would be attractive to buyers? If you can then maybe the flea market is for you.

Craft and Art Shows

Art and craft shows can be a lot of fun and hard work. They are very similar to doing farmers and flea markets and can as simple as a single table, to elaborate and heavily decorated booths.

There are two types of shows to be aware of, juried and non-juried. A non-juried show is a show that is open to everyone as long as the spaces are available. These shows tend to be less expensive to participate in.

A juried show is one that those wishing to participate must pass a jury examination. The Jury will be looking at your booth design, the product you sell, the number of other artist that are similar to you, and the availability of space. Most juried shows will require a booth setup. Juried shows are usually more expensive and require larger investments.

The plus side to the higher cost is that juried shows tend to be well publicized and have been around for years. The juried shows seem to attract larger groups of customer than non-juried shows.

Many people enjoy working the art and craft show circuit. If this is something you might enjoy check out these resources.

Berman Graphics

Art Fair Calendar   www.artfaircalendar.com

Card Parties

What is a Card Party you ask? This idea came from a competitor in the town I reside in and I thought it is a great idea. This enterprising individual cleaned out their garage and sent out invitations to as many people they knew to come to the card party.

The invitation read that the party was to help determine this year's holiday offering. Guest were asked to pick which cards would go to the printers and which didn't make the cut. The invitations also stated that there would be refreshments and door prizes, including a flat screen television.

Attendance was good and I am sure many cards were sold that day. Besides It was a party and a lot of fun.

You can be as elaborate as you wish when setting up your party. Some items you might consider are:

- Location?

- How many card samples should I show?

- How many people should I invite?

- Door Prizes?

- If so what prizes should I advertise?

- Should I have food?

- Should I offer wine?

- How long should the party last?

- Do I have enough parking space?

- What day is best?

- What time is best?

As always, plan your party. With a good plan in place you could have a successful party.

If this sounds like something that you might benefit from, then be all means give it your best shot.

Create a Card Club via Direct Mail

Just this week my wife received in the mail an invitation to join a card club. The envelope included four cards and envelopes, an eleven by seventeen printed on both sides brochure, return envelope, and return card for payment. Upon receipt of payment, every six to eight she would receive a package of ten cards with envelopes and bookmarks. What a great idea.

To set up a direct mail campaign like the one above takes planning. Some areas to consider when making a direct mail plan are:

- List selection

- Postage

- Print material

- Printing Cost

- Mailing Timing

- Fulfillment

- Tracking All the Variables

You can chose to go about setting up a direct mail campaign by your self. In today's data driven world it is not all that difficult. You can also hire someone or company that will do almost all the work for you. You can decide how much of the job you can do and how much to farm out.

The most important part of any direct mail plan is the list. The best list is the one you have captured from your site and social media pages. These people have already expressed an interest in what you do and sell. The next best is a list that you purchase from a list broker. Info USA is probably the most well know in the list area. Info USA will give you many choices to help sort out your list to target the best possible candidate for your campaign.

Know your customer. It is difficult to buy a list that will produce results if you do not know what to look for in a customer. A customer profile will help in sorting through the names to get a list that can produce enough sales to make a profit.

Creating a customer profile is not as hard as it sounds. Just ask your customers about themselves. What? Use an online survey company to ask customers about themselves. Learn where they shop, what kind of foods do they like, what do they read, and the questions can go on and on. Try to keep your survey short. Try not to take up more than five minutes and for best results offer a gift. The gift can be something they can download such as an e book.

What do you put in your direct mail package? The answer to that question depends on your budget. At the very least your package needs to include the following:

- Opening letter
- Free cards and envelopes
- Return card
- Return postage paid envelope
- A brochure describing your offer
- The outside envelope

Research all of the items above until you are comfortable with their uses. One way to learn about direct mail is to study the advertisements that you receive. Pay attention to how the packet of information is assembled. Notice all the items that are included with the offer. If you study what direct mail that is sent to you, I promise you will quickly learn how to prepare your own direst mail offer.

Base your offer on a theme. Themes help you target your efforts. If you sell cards that feature horses, then you know your list should be geared towards horse loving folks.

The direct mail market is a lot like marketing on the internet in that all efforts can be tested and measured. Testing and measuring is the key to success. Each part of a campaign can be measured and scaled. Once you have determined that a campaign is successful it is very easy to scale and bring in more sales.

The biggest disadvantage of a direct mail campaign is the up front cost to establish the campaign. The United States post office will make you pay for your postage at the time of delivery. There is also the printer and list supplier, which also get paid at the time the service is performed. The price per individual piece may not sound to expensive, but multiply that by a couple of thousand and you have a rather large investment.

If starting a direct mail business with your cards sounds exciting to you, then by all means go for it. There is a plethora of information on direct marketing via mail. Continue to research the subject and you could be the next card club.

Corporate Sales

I recently had outpatient surgery at a local hospital. It was an in and out procedure and I was home the same day. Two days later I received a card in the mail from the nurses' station at the hospital. It was a simple card that stated they were hopeful for a full recovery and they were glad to have been my nurse. It had been hand addresses and signed by the nurses. The card I received was produced by a local card creator.

I tell this story to show that what I mean by "corporate sales." There are thousands of companies that are in need of these types of cards, and they could be buying them from you.

To cultivate sales in this area, a network is a valuable resource. The more people you associate with the greater your chance of making these kinds of sales. Be prepared with a line of cards that can be used in a corporate setting and most of all don't be afraid to ask questions.

The best type of card to start with in corporate sales is a thank you card. If you are designing a card for a corporate client, try to think like their customers think. For example, a thank you card for an automotive repair might would have a car theme to it but same card would not work a cleaning service.

Corporate sales can one of the most profitable areas of card production. Many people tend not to work this area of sales because it requires a lot of one on one attention and you may have to create a card just for a specific client. The plus side of the equation is that once you have completed the creation and made the sale, you are a great position to be that companies card supplier. Reorders are a beautiful!

Wholesale

Florist

Florist are a wonderful place to start you greeting card wholesale accounts. Cards and flowers just go together. I was in the wholesale floral distribution business for over thirty years and I know that florist consume a lot of greeting cards.

Before attempting to sell to a florist I suggest that you visit several to get a feel for how they operate and the types of products that you may create that fit in with their stores.

Sympathy is a large part of many florists, and it would be wise to have several sympathy cards in your line.

Love is another part of a florist business. There are many types of cards to fit this need, make sure yours fit in with the overall feel of the shop.

Florist are also a good place to sell boxed sets. Try adding a ribbon to your boxed sets to help them stand out.

When I was selling to florist I offered to put the name of the shop on the back of my cards. Doing this helped me stand out from all the out of town vendors. The shop owners liked this feature and helped me sell more cards.

Many florist may already have displays in the store just waiting for your cards. Be prepared to offer help in providing display if they do not have any open spaces. Many types of displays work well in florist settings.

When making contact with a florist, in most cases you will be dealing with the owner. Be sure to follow the rules of selling and be respectful of your client's time.

Dog Groomers

There are two ways to make a sale with a dog groomer. The first way to sell cards in the dog groomer market is to offer thank you cards the groomer sends to their clients. Everyone loves getting a thank you card.

When selling thank-you cards to groomers it is wise to stress the importance of customer relationships and that your thank you cards are the perfect way of keeping those relationships' happy.

The second way a dog groomer can help with your wholesale greeting card business is to offer cards for sell to their customers. Remember that this is a wholesaling opportunity, and treat it as such. Remind the potential clients that they will make money off of each sale.

Pet and Feed Stores

Pet stores are quite different than groomers. A pet store may have a love of animals, but they are in business to make money selling many items, and this is good news for card makers. Pet and feed stores are like any other retail business.

A card line for the pet and feed business can be diverse. They are many kinds of themes and art work that can be used for your card line. Animals, flowers, landscapes and farm scenes will sell well. Sympathy cards for animals of all types may sell well at a pet and feed store.

Be prepared to offer display in stores. A floor spinner works well in most of these locations.

If your pet and feed store are part of a chain then skip ahead to the section on dealing with chain stores. If it is a single store with one owner then this is the person you will want to do business with. In dealing with any retain store stress that your products will help increase their profits.

Veterinarian

A veterinarian is one of those prospective clients that can be a dual source of sales. You can offer cards to their clients and maybe be the provider of cards that the vet sends to their customers. The situation is very similar to dog groomers, with the exception that you may have more space to display your cards

Veterinarians have to be masters at customer relationships and your cards can help them achieve better communications with their clients. Stress this when meeting with the office manger at the veterinarian's place of business.

When making contact at a veterinarian's office you will most likely have a two person sale to make. The first sale is to the office manger. You must convince the office manger that you have the cards that will fit their needs. Once you have convinced the office manger you may or may not have to then convince the Veterinarian.

I believe that doing business with a veterinarian can be a great long term relationship. This kind of business can result in many years of sales.

Restaurants

Restaurants can be a tough sell. Space in a restaurant can be limited. Restaurant owners sell food and service, they know very little about the greeting card business. Education is the key to having your cards in a restaurant. It is best to have a definite plan before approaching a restaurant owner.

Space is limited at many restaurants, so think out your display options before trying to make a sale. In many cases a floor spinner will do a nice job. You may also want to consider a small counter top display.

Many restaurants today have a theme associated with there food selection. Be mindful of the theme when choosing which to cards to place in the restaurant.

Unless your restaurant is a chain you will be dealing with the owner. Make sure to avoid their busy times during the day. Nothing will make an owner mad is to interrupt them when they are busy.

Gas stations

When I was a kid growing up, the only items you would find in a gas station where wiper blades, oil cans, and a gumball machine. That is no longer the situation any more. Many of today's gas stations are more like small stores that just happen to sell gasoline.

The gas stations I am referring to in this section are the single or small chain stations. There is a entirely different process with dealing with large chain type stations. In small and single owned stations you will be dealing with the owner or someone very close to the owner. In the large chain stations there is a designated buyer for items other than gasoline, and you skip ahead to dealing with chain stores section.

Dealing with the owner of small gas stations leaves open many possibilities to insert your greeting cards into their product mix. Many types of display options and variety of cards can be sold at gas stations. As opposed to dealing with a restaurant owner, dealing with a small gas station owner is best done by first asking questions. Learn what space they have available and what level of service do they expect.

Once you have learned about the gas station company, formulate a plan that would best fit their style of business. If you plan right and follow the rules of selling you should be able to place you greeting card in their product mix.

Convenience Store

Many convenience stores are locally owned and this is great news for the industrious card seller. Being local means that you have a better chance of dealing with an owner and making a sale.

When dealing with a convenience store owner remember that most convenience stores have their layouts carefully planned. Have a couple of display options available. There are many types of displays that might work; ask questions.

A wide variety of cards may be sold in a convenience store. If you produce cards with a local taste a convenience store is a great place to offer your products.

Drug Stores

Independently owned drug stores are another great place to wholesale you cards. Many times these stores have been part the community for many years, and are already accustomed to doing business with local vendors. Drug stores also sell a variety of products and will already have cards to sell. If you are a local vendor you have the advantage of being able to service your cards on a regular schedule.

Drug stores have been selling greeting cards for a long time. You will not be the first to try to make a sale to them. Make sure your cards stand out from all the others. If local landmarks are some of the types of cards you produce then you have a product that will stand out. Local drug stores love to promote local vendors.

Display in a drug store can be different then in many other retail locations. Most drug stores have at least one card vendor and the vendor may own the display used for their cards. You will not be able to use their display if this is the case. You need to have some display options ready. As with any sale it is best to ask questions and learn what type of display space is available that will work for you and the customer.

You can sell a wide variety of cards at the local drug store. I would suggest to have a nice selection of get well and happy birthday cards. These categories along with thinking of you cards sell well at the local drug store.

Gift Shops

There are two types of gifts shops. The first is non-profit and the other is for profit. Both types of shops can be a good fit for your wholesale card company.

Dealing with a non-profit gift shop may be a little harder to sell than a shop for profit. To make a sale to a non-profit shop you may have to present your product several times to get to the buyer. Many times the buyer for a non-profit is not just one person but a board of people.

Most non-profit gift shops operate with a limited budget. To help guarantee a sale to anon-profit offer your cards on consignment. Many non-profits make very little profit and have limited funds to purchase new items for sale. Your cards on consignment will help provide quality products and help keep down costs.

Dealing with a for profit gift shop can be just as challenging. Many of today's gift are run by big chain store type companies but not all. If you are lucky enough to have a gift shop that has a single owner then your chances of getting your product into their stores is better. Remember that every card company in the world wants to be their shop, and you are just another vendor. Think local to help you stand out from the crowd.

The enterprising Card seller realizes that they are but one of many and has a plan to stand out. There many ways to stand out above most. Use all the reasons you came come up with to convince the owner that your cards are the fit for their store.

Display in gifts shops can be varied. Many of the shops might already have displays. Work with the shop manger or owner to decide which type of displays you have to work with.

Gifts shops are a good place to sell all types of cards. If you produce artsy type cards then you may a prefect fit for the gift shop business. Boxed sets also sell well in a gift shop setting.

Arts Councils

Arts Council growth has exploded over the last twenty years; chances are there is one near you. I highly recommend that you join. They are usually not too expensive.

Many of today's Arts Councils have gifts shops that represent their membership. If you are a member then you have a pretty good chance of having your cards for sale in their gift shop. Contact the director or a board member to find out how to go about placing your cards in the store. Be prepared to provide display and you will most likely be providing your cards on consignment. Make sure to keep up with the cards you place there and be willing to keep you cards neat and seasonal.

Book Stores

Book stores are flooded with vendors selling all kinds of products. Their situation is very similar to gifts shops.

Dealing with a book store owner is the same as dealing with the gift shop owner. You have to find a way to stand out from the crowd. Local greeting cards are one way of standing out from the crowd.

Boxed sets and single card sales are possible at book stores. Display in these store may be provided or you may have to provide your own displays. If possible a floor spinner works best.

ℤ✑   A word about selling local

When I was a young man at my first job, the owner of the company told me that a business cannot survive if it does not have the business in its backyard. This was said before the age of globalization, but it still carries some weight today. Your local community is still the best place to start your wholesale greeting card company. Some the advantages of selling local are:

- You may already know some of your prospects

- You can offer a level of service that is hard to match by out of town suppliers

- You can offer you product on consignment

- You can help promote their business

- You can save the prospect money by offering free delivery (remember you live here)

- You can save the prospect time by offering to set up your display

- You can respond very quickly to any requests

You can see that there are many benefits to selling local, but the biggest benefit is that you are available to service your product, keep it clean and up to date with the seasons. Most small retail business owners are very busy people with more to do in a day then they can get done, you can save them time and money. Make sure you stress this fact with every chance you get. Your level of service may be the biggest difference between you and the competition.

When selling to local companies consider the possibility of helping them promote your products. Perhaps you can share the cost of advertising.

Selling local also gives you faster feedback. You will know quicker than out of town vendors if a product is not preforming well, and can do something about it. This also works in the reverse. You will quickly know if you need to make more of a product if it sells well.

Just these two benefits of selling local should be enough to convince you that the best place to start your wholesale greeting card business is your own backyard.

Selling on the World Wide Web

The world wide web has brought about many new ways to sell greeting cards. Some people have made their business by selling entirely on the web. I have never been a big believer in putting all my eggs in one basket so I divide my time between selling both online and off. One the exciting areas about the web is that you can cultivate a world wide audience. There are billions of potential customers and that can be exciting.

Methods of selling on the web

There are two methods of filling orders for the web. One method is where you fulfill the orders. You create, sell, package, and deliver you product to the post office. Another method of fulfilling orders is called print on demand. Print on Demand is when you sell the product but another company prints, packages, and delivers your product to the customer and in many cases they collect the money.

Promotion on the world wide web

One the most difficult areas of the web is promotion. There are thousands of choices to make and some can cost a lot of money. I have yet to find the magic formula that brings in sales.

The biggest mistake that I have made in my online marketing efforts is not having a plan. I thought that if I had a website and a few Google ads that the world would be flying to me for their greeting card needs. Not true. Not even close. The best I did was waste my valuable money. Research and planing are the most valuable money and time you can invest.

It is beyond the scope of this book to cover all the possible marketing opportunities. The web moves very fast and requires a diligent effort to keep up with all the changes. As soon as this book is published, the information would be obsolete. If web marketing is important to you then study everyday to keep up with the changes.

The website is home base for most of your online marketing, before we can continue, you need to decide what type of website you are trying to create. Do you want only wholesale customer? Are your sales directed to the end user? Or maybe somewhere in-between? Each type of site requires a different type of approach. Let us take a look at the items that are similar.

Before we go on I would like to recommend that you have your files organized. It is much easier to work on the web if you have a system of organizing your files. A good system will save you lots of time and headaches.

Web work also requires that you have the best possible photos of you work as possible. Remember that the web is visual medium and photos are the heartbeat of a good web presence. Do not cut corners in this area.

Setting a website for wholesale only is somewhat different then a site set up for the end user. If you are selling to both the end user and to a wholesale customer you might want to consider a password to enter the wholesale side of the site.

A customer profile is must, regardless of what type of site you set up. You can not be everything to everybody. Learn who your end customers are and what they are interested in. This step may take some time and require some research. You need to ask lots of questions. Questions like:

- Are my customers male or female?

- What ages are my customers?

- What background do my customers have?

- What ethnicity are my customers?

- Where do my customer like to hang out?

- What kind of foods do my customer care for?

- What are the hobbies of my customers?

Take time to answer these questions. Do not guess! When you know the answers to questions like the ones above, you have a much better chance of targeting you promotions to the right people. Yea, I know this all sounds so elementary, but many producers fail to do this and then wonder why they can not make any sales.

If you have more than just a single line of cards to sell this step of customer profiling must be done for each of the lines. In fact I have begun to ask the questions listed above for each single card I make. What good is a card that no body wants?

If you are selling strictly wholesale, then a customer profile needs to be done for each prospect that you want to sell to.

Another big difference from selling on the web versus selling to stores is face time. When you are trying to wholesale your cards to companies you will end up face to face with the potential client. When selling on the web you most likely will never see the person buying your cards. This can make selling on the web challenging and requires that you make your site as personable as possible.

Make your site a reflection of yourself. Learn the skills necessary that makes your site a warm and friendly place to do business. Make it easy for people to purchase. You have heard it before but I will say it again, keep it simple.

With a well thought out website and a good customer profile you have a way to maximize your marketing efforts. You drive the right type of prospect to your door and have a good chance of making a sale.

Now let us look at some companies that help drive prospects and make sales.

🖐️🖐️ You Fulfill the orders

ETSY

ETSY is currently the worlds marketplace for handmade goods. I think the latest numbers can explain just how big Etsy is:

- 36 million items for sales

- 22.6 million buyers

- 1.5 million sellers

- 1.93 billion in sales

  If you sell handmade cards then, Etsy is the place to be.

  Setting up your store in Etsy is easy and does not take a lot of computer skills. You can easily have your store up and running in as little as fifteen minutes. However take time to explore all the possibilities. The power of Etsy, just like Amazon, is a robust selling platform. I suggest that you go through each item on the platform and check it out. I am sure you will find many useful properties for your business.

  Etsy allows you to set your own prices. I find this a benefit over most of the commission types sites. I prefer to be in charge of my pricing.

  Etsy has an active marking program to help promote your shop. Etsy badges is a program that lets you embed a distinctive mark called a badge on your website,blog or social media page. When someone clicks on this badge they are directed to your Etsy store. The direction to embed a badge on your site is easy to follow and does not take a lot of time. Etsy also has a coupon program that is easy to use. Again Etsy makes it easy. Just follow the directions and you will have coupons for your products.

Etsy also has for selected vendors a wholesale program that may get you into large chain stores. This is a feature that as far as I know is only available through the Etsy platform. For those vendors that can supply large quantities of product and have met the Etsy conditions, Etsy provides a place and venue to showcase their products to upscale chain stores. This is a feature that is worth checking into if you want to be a supplier to some of Americas upscale stores.

Etsy is a E commerce platform that removes most of the hassle of processing payments. Setting up this part of your store is not difficult but may require a little more then a few minutes.

Etsy does most of the marketing and payment processing for very cost but it does cost. Etsy charges a listing fee. The fees are not much on each item; most of the time under a dollar. However they can add up if you are not paying attention. Be careful and test every item to see which items are money makers.

Etsy support is easy to find and contains tons of useful information. I would start with the sellers handbook. There is also many books and blogs on the subject of Etsy selling.

Amazon Handmade

The new contender in the market is Amazon handmade. At the time of this writing Amazon had just announced that it would be entering the world of hand made goods. One of the immediate benefits of dealing with Amazon is the power of their marketing platform. In order to use this powerful platform you must be approved by the Amazon Handmade Team. Once approved, set up is easy and straight forward.

At the time of this writing Amazon offers two types of selling plans. Individual and professional. Check out the site to see which type of account fits your needs. If you registrar as an individual account you are limited to forty items or less. Professional accounts can sell more items but there is thirty nine dollar a month fee. Set up for the individual account is free and is not difficult.

When setting your prices make sure you understand the fees involved. Amazon charges referral fees and processing fees. Explore the Amazon platform and see how others are handling the site including the custom order features.

We have yet to see any numbers from Amazon but I am sure they are going to make an impact on the market place. If selling to mufti-national audience excites you then be all means sign up and participate with Amazon Handmade. You can always say that your cards are available in the worlds largest retailer.

Your own web site

Let's face it, you most likely already have your own website.

You have been working on drawing visitors to your site with valuable content. It is only natural that you would want to offer you cards for sale and there are many ways to do so.

The easiest way to offer your cards for sale is to use one the sites listed above. Etsy and Amazon have badges that you can embed to your site. You can also link a card picture to your store. I have used both methods successfully. Test, test,test.

There is a group of marketers that say you lose sales when a visitor clicks on a product and is directed to another site. In other words they say you should keep the visitor on your site as long as possible. Keeping a visitor on your site is now a lot easier than it use to be just a few years ago. Just do a search for companies that will let you process payments easily through your site and you will find there are many to chose from.

There are pros and cons to selling from your website and one of the biggest cons is the time it takes to put together the site. Think hard before you set on selling products from your site. A plan to sell from the site is a must. Decide how much of the work you can do and how much needs to be farmed out. Make it as easy as possible for a visitor to purchase from you.

The pro factor is a big one. The possible sale is already on your site. They are there now. If you have made it easy for them to purchase, and they are already interested, then you have a great chance of making a sale.

Many of today's website providers include an e-commerce platform with their web offerings. If you do not already have a website then you might want to consider a company that does provide such a service before committing.

It is possible to produce sales from your own website. It takes planing, designing, writing and producing an enjoyable experience for the visitor. When you get all areas of your site running smoothly you can enjoy the benefits of sales.

Facebook

When Facebook first started many people hailed its ability to promote their products. Facebook was the place to tell the your friends all about what you are up to. Today's internet will allow you to set up a store on your personal and company Facebook page. The company that comes to mind when trying to set up a store on Facebook is Shopify.

Shopify can integrate with your Facebook page or in your own website. The platform is easy to set up and get running. Shopify provides display and descriptions and payment processing. Shopify will offer you a thirty day free trail to see if you will benefit from their service.

For many people Shopify and a Facebook page is all you need to sell your greeting cards but remember Facebook is still the place to promote your business.

Someone Else fulfills the orders

In this section I look at a few companies that offer fulfillment services. In this segment there are two types of services that should be aware of. First services that I look at are companies that pay a commission on sales but let you set the price, and the second pays commission but they set the prices. Each of these business models seem to be successful. Let us take a closer look.

Greeting Card Universe

When I first started selling cards on the web I found Greeting Card Universe. (GCU) When I first joined they had less the fifty thousand cards and I made sales. As of this writing they have over six hundred thousand cards. Getting noticed in the crowd became a lot harder.

The price of greeting cards for is set by GCU. They pay the artist a commission on the sale of each that has sold. In the beginning they paid a nice commission on their sales but now the commission has fallen to just a few pennies on a sale.

Greeting Card Universe provides a free store front to all it's customers. It is easy to set up and you can be online in minutes. Each store front has two galleries. One gallery is for the public to view. The second gallery is called a private and it is only shown to those prospects that click on the private gallery tab. The public gallery can be searched by the search bar. The private gallery is not part of the public search. There is no limit to the number of cards you can submit. There is a screening process that you must go through, on every card submitted to be available for the public to purchase. If your card is not approved for the public you can still offer the card through your private gallery.

Once your cards have been approved for sale to the public, GCU will set the price. You have none to very little control of the price GCU charges for a card. GCU pay a commission for each of your cards sold. The amount they pay is small and for many is not worth the time. GCU also will run sales on cards and the amount they pay gets even smaller.

If you have ever wanted to have your cards available in Target stores then GCU may be for you. GCU at the time of this writing has a deal with Target to print the cards and make them available at the customers local Target store. For many sellers this is a great service.

GCU also allows for a customer to personalize the cards they purchase. Cards that you submit must have a blank space for the customer to add their message. When uploading your images GCU provides a online template that helps you know what part of the cards is left for personalization. This is an added benefit that you can promote when trying to sell your cards online.

Greeting Card Universe offers the greeting card producer a complete package. Selling, printing, and payment collection, along with options for delivery, make GCU a company that can handle all your needs.

Zazzle, Cafe Press and others

There are many companies that offer the greeting card producer a way to sell their products. If your cards can be printed and do not require that each be handled with embellishments then one of these companies could be just right for you.

Most of these companies sell more than just greeting cards. They off a wide variety of products that you can create. This can be great news for many producers. Coffee mugs, tee shirts, journals, coasters, note pads are just a few of the items that your can have your images printed on.

These companies provide a free store front and make their money from the products you sell. They provide the producer a base price for the products they sell. When you load an item to sell, they provide the base price and you then can add to the selling price the amount of profit you prefer to make. I like this system better then something like GCU where I have no control over the price.

All of these companies have a search-able database of products and sellers. With a little luck you may show up in a search result.

If you want to offer more then just a greeting card to your customers then I suggest you look into one of these companies.

Fine Art America

The last company I want to discuss is Fine Art America. I like this company and I use it on all my sites including Facebook. Fine Art America was set up to service photographers and artist who wanted to sell their prints. Greeting cards and other items have been added as the site grew.

Fine Art America (FAA) charges a fee for their service, and it in my opinion is reasonable. The fee allows you to integrate FAA with your website and Facebook page. The fee also will allow you to participate in their print on demand service.

One of the reasons I like FAA is that you can sell using their print on demand service and sell one of a kind handmade products. You do not have to pay the fee to sell one of a kind products, but you will not be able to use the integration services.

FAA allows you to set your own prices. As I have mentioned before I like to be in control of my prices. Just like Zazzle, Cafe Press, and others FAA has a base price for their products and you can then add your markup.

FAA offers several options for helping the producer market their products. The option I like the best, is the ability to print high quality sales sheets right from your computer. These sales sheets can help you make sales to your off line customers and are easy to produce.

If you want to sell fine art prints and greeting cards then Fine Art America is a great company to do business with. I highly recommend that you investigate the company and it's services.

Chain Stores

When I first started to write this book on where and how to sell greeting cards I included chain stores. with the mass merchandisers I found that this wrong. There are differences between the two types of retailers.

Mass merchandisers have a structure that all stores report to one main entity. They have one corporate owner. But chain stores do not always have one owner. Chain store can be a sole proprietary, family owned, or have a closely held corporation own them. Chain stores can be as small as three or as large as hundreds. Many of the chains are local and some may be regional.

Another difference that I noticed is that chains stores tend to make the bulk of their money selling one item. A gas station chain makes most of it's sales through gasoline. A Drug store chain sells drugs to make their money. This does not mean that the chain store does not make money on all the items they sell, just that the core monies come from one product. Mass merchandisers make their money selling everything under the sun.

Dealing with chains stores requires that you do some research. Learn the levels of management that the chain store has. Some large chain stores are set up like the mass merchandisers. Some are small and operate with one or two people calling all the shots. Ask the mangers at the stores you are interested in doing business with, about who to see to sell your cards. Most of the time the mangers can send you in the right direction.

Once you have found the buyer it is important that you have a plan . Most of these buyers are very busy and it pays to be ready. Not only do you need to present your cards you may have to also sell the idea of having cards at all. Be prepared to talk numbers. Tell them how much money they can make. Explain to the buyer the value that you can bring to the table.

Dealing with a chain store in your area may allow you to keep warehouse inventory levels lower. The requirements to do business with a smaller chain may be easier to comply with. So, again I can not emphasis enough to do your research.

When planing to sell to a chain store consider what type of display would be best suited for the stores layout. In many cases a small floor spinner will work out best. Taylor your card offerings and theme to match the type of business you are selling to.

Growing your business with sales to a small chain store can be very exciting. Doing business with just one small chain store can catapult your sales. Do not be timid just because they are chain store, go out and look for those opportunities!

Mass Merchandisers

I am sure that there are many of us that would love to be a provider to one of the mass merchandisers or large box stores. Questions that you need to ask yourself before thinking about doing business with one of the large companies are:

- Can I produce enough product?

- Can I wait thirty or sixty days before getting paid?

- How will I maintain quality of my product?

- Who provides display?

- Does my product have a mass appeal?

Where Do you start? First you must meet the requirements that theses types of stores have. Requirements vary from merchandisers. Those that I have tried to sell to, list their requirements for vendors somewhere on their websites. Notice that I said somewhere on the site, you may have to search around to find the correct page.

Once you have decided that you can meet the requirements of the merchandiser, the next step is to identify the buyer of greeting cards. This may require a phone call to the headquarters. The buyer may also be listed in the company directory.

Making contact with the correct person is the first step in selling to mass merchandiser. These are usually very busy people, so be ready to make your first pitch as soon as you get them on the phone. Hopefully you can get an appointment to see them and make a presentation.

Before you make a pitch to a mass merchandiser you need to learn the language of the buyer. Mass merchandisers talk in terms like sales per square foot, inventory turnover, and seasonal cycles. Know the answers to these questions. Research until you are comfortable with these terms and can talk their language.

If you get the chance to make a sales pitch to a buyer at a mass merchandiser, do not waste their time. Have samples ready and make sure you know the answers to their questions. Remember theses are professional buyers and are not easily fooled. They know what they can sell and if you fit into what they want then you may become one of their vendors. It can be done!

When I was a young man I had an idea that I thought would sell well in a mass market type store. I did not meet their requirements but I thought I would give a try anyway. Here is that story.

After about a month of asking questions, I finally had identified the buyer of a large mass merchandiser and made an appointment to meet with him. Great I thought, step one completed.

My appointment was for four in the afternoon and I arrived just a few minutes early. I entered the building and talked with the receptionist. She informed me that the buyer I needed to see was busy and would be with me as soon as possible. After about a thirty minute wait the buyer came to the door and escorted me to his desk. It was a very large room with a hundred or so desks lined up in rows. We were in the middle. He sat back in his chair and said "so what are you here to sell me."

I was ready for that question and began my sales pitch. It only took me a couple of minutes to explain what I was selling and how I would go about servicing my products. He said nothing. I then explained how I was going to make the company money, better yet a profit and how I was going to make him look good. Much to my surprise his response was, "sounds good when can we get started." "How about next week." I said. "Good, we will start with store number xzy" I can not begin to explain the joy of that moment. I felt like I had just climbed to the mountain top.

The next week I arrived with my product and display stand at xyz store. Excited, I located the store manger and introduced myself. The store manger was much less excited then I was and told me to wait while he checked out my story. Thirty or forty minutes latter she came out of office and said " John (buyer at the main office) said I had to give you a try." She then showed me some out of the way place, where I could set my display and present my product. This was the same at every store I went to. I became a little less excited.

One of the selling points that used to convince the buyer to do business with me was that I would service the product and maintain the quality, just like the bread and milk people. I would also take care of any seasonal changes. Big mistake. The mass merchandiser that I was dealing with had a workforce that was part of a union. Since I serviced my own products the union members did not care for me. As far as they were concerned I was taking work that they should be doing. They thought that I was stealing their jobs.

It only took about nine months for me to realize that I was fighting a losing battle. My product never got a chance. I was under capitalized and it showed.

Now I understand why these mass merchandisers have the requirements to do business with them, perhaps if I had met the requirements I might have had a better chance.

If you have dreams of being a provider to mass merchandiser, then by all means give it your best shot, all they can say is no!

Made in the USA
Columbia, SC
07 January 2020